I Am a Fish

The Life of a Clown Fish

by Darlene R. Stille illustrated by Todd Ouren

Special thanks to our advisers for their expertise:

Susan H. Shane, Ph.D., Biology
University of California at Santa Cruz

Susan Kesselring, M.A., Literacy Educator
Rosemount-Apple Valley-Eagan (Minnesota) School District

I Live in the Ocean

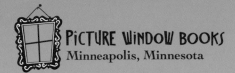

PICTURE WINDOW BOOKS
Minneapolis, Minnesota

Managing Editors: Bob Temple, Catherine Neitge
Creative Director: Terri Foley
Editors: Nadia Higgins, Patricia Stockland
Editorial Adviser: Andrea Cascardi
Designer: Todd Ouren
Page production: Picture Window Books
The illustrations in this book were prepared digitally.

Picture Window Books
5115 Excelsior Boulevard
Suite 232
Minneapolis, MN 55416
877-845-8392
www.picturewindowbooks.com

Printed in the United States of America.

Library of Congress Cataloging-in-Publication Data
Stille, Darlene R.
I am a fish : the life of a clown fish / by Darlene R. Stille ;
illustrated by Todd Ouren.
p. cm. — (I live in the ocean)
Includes bibliographical references (p.   ).
ISBN 1-4048-0595-8 (reinforced lib. bdg.)
1. Anemonefishes—Juvenile literature. I. Ouren, Todd, ill.
II. Title.

QL638.P77S75 2004
597'.72—dc22   2004000886

I wriggle my tail. I swish my fins. I am a fish that lives in the ocean.

Look at my stripes. They call me a clown fish. Do I look like I'm wearing a costume?

The clown fish is a tiny tropical fish. Tropical fish live in warm salt water.

3

I am only as long as your hand is wide, about 2 inches. My body is thin and smaller at both ends. My body's special shape is just right for sliding through the sea.

A clown fish moves its tail from side to side to move through the ocean.

4

As I swim, I take big gulps of water. The water passes over the gills on the sides of my head. The gills let me breathe under water.

My colors are pretty, aren't they? They help me, too.

I'm colorful because I live in a colorful place. My bright body helps me blend in. Big, hungry fish can't spot me as I swim by.

6

A clown fish's colors come from its scales. These are little bony plates that cover and protect a fish's body.

This beautiful ocean garden is called a coral reef. It's made from the stony shells of tiny coral animals. The shells piled up over thousands and thousands of years.

It takes billions of coral animals to make a reef. Only the corals on the outer layer of the reef are alive. When they die, their shells will add to the pile.

I have lots of neighbors here. They're just as colorful as I am. People come from all around the world to watch us swim in our amazing reef.

Come and meet my very best friend, a sea anemone. (You say it "ah-NEM-uh-nee.") An anemone looks like a plant, doesn't it? It's really an animal with lots of swaying tentacles.

My anemone friend and I live together on the reef. You could call us reef mates!

An anemone looks like a plant, so fish think it is harmless. These fish are actually prey for the anemone.

11

My friend has stinging tentacles, but they don't bother me. I glide by them and don't feel a thing.

When other fish get close, the anemone stings them with its tentacles. It pulls the fish into its mouth. I get to eat the leftovers. Yum!

A clown fish is covered with special slime, or mucus. This mucus coating is probably what keeps it safe from an anemone's stinging tentacles.

Clown fish are also known as anemone fish.

I help my friend, too. We keep each other safe. I chase its enemies away. When one of my enemies gets close, I hide between the anemone's tentacles.

I share my anemone friend with four other clown fish. They all know that I'm the boss. I am the female and the biggest clown fish here.

Like all clown fish, I was a male when I was born.
When I became the biggest fish in my group,
I turned into a female. Now I can have babies.

Many kinds of tropical
fish change from female
to male. Clown fish are
unusual because they
go from male to female.

My mate is the second biggest fish here. He makes a nest under the anemone's tentacles. This is for our eggs.

I can lay 1,000 eggs at a time. My mate guards the eggs until the babies hatch.

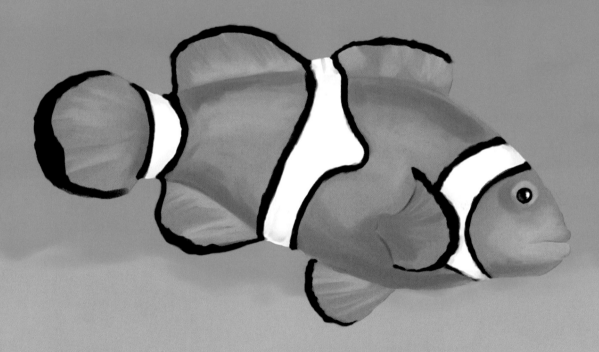

The male takes good care of the eggs. He cleans the nest. He fans the eggs with his body to keep fresh water flowing over them.

19

After our babies hatch, they will live for a while at the surface of the ocean. As they drift on the waves, they will eat and get bigger, just like I did when I was younger.

A clown fish may live from six to 10 years.

When they grow up, they will find their own anemone friends and start their own families in this beautiful sea garden.

A Clown Fish's Amazing Body

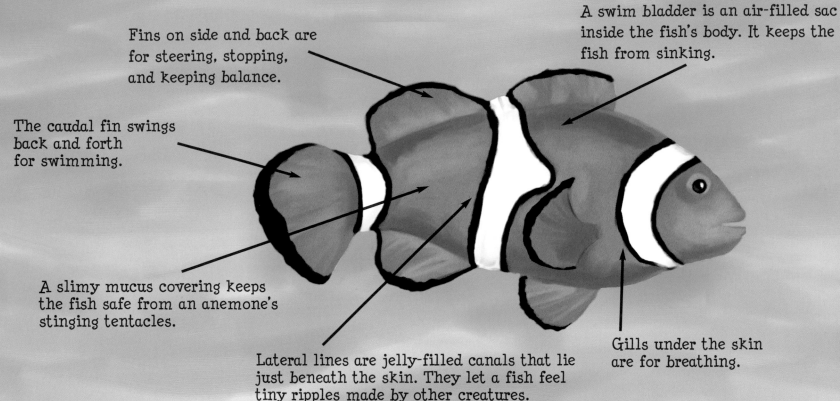

Fins on side and back are for steering, stopping, and keeping balance.

A swim bladder is an air-filled sac inside the fish's body. It keeps the fish from sinking.

The caudal fin swings back and forth for swimming.

A slimy mucus covering keeps the fish safe from an anemone's stinging tentacles.

Lateral lines are jelly-filled canals that lie just beneath the skin. They let a fish feel tiny ripples made by other creatures.

Gills under the skin are for breathing.

Fun Facts

All Kinds of Fish

There are about 25,000 species (or kinds) of fish. Fish come in all sizes. Some fish look like snakes. Some fish look like rocks. Rays are fish that look like kites with tails.

Fish Everywhere

Fish can live in almost any type of water. Some live in the pitch-black darkness at the bottom of the ocean. Some live in the near-freezing water of the Arctic. There are even fish that can live in a dried-out riverbed for months at a time.

How Old Are You?

The first fish appeared on Earth about 500 million years ago. Fish were the first animals with backbones.

Always Wide-Eyed
Fish don't have eyelids. They can rest with their eyes open. Since they never leave water, their eyes never get dry.

 Icky Who?
Scientists who study fish are called ichthyologists (IHK-thee-OL-uh-jihsts).

 Body Clues
You can tell how a fish moves by how it looks. If a fish has skinny fins and a narrow tail, it probably swims fast. A fish with a wide, square tail can't swim as fast, but it can move easily around rocks and reefs.

My Coral Reef Neighbors

blue-face angelfish

bannerfish

butterfly fish

Glossary

anemone—an ocean animal that looks like a plant; anemones eat other sea creatures

coral reef—billions of shells of tiny coral animals that make up a ridge in the ocean; coral reefs are found in warm, shallow parts of oceans

gills—openings on the sides of a fish's head; gills take oxygen out of water to let a fish breathe

mucus—a slimy substance that coats a fish's skin

tentacle—long, bendable body parts that animals such as anemones and octopuses have instead of arms; tentacles are for touching and grabbing things

tropical—animals and plants that live in warm places near Earth's equator

To Learn More

At the Library

Boyle, Doe, and Steven Petruccio (Illustrator). *Coral Reef Hideaway : The Story of a Clown Anemonefish*. Norwalk, Conn.: Soundprints, 1995.

Schaefer, Lola M. *Sea Anemones (Ooey-Gooey Animals)*. Chicago: Heinemann Library, 2002.

Spicer, Maggee, and Richard Thompson. *Fishes in the Ocean*. Toronto: Fitzhenry & Whiteside, 2001.

On the Web

FactHound offers a safe, fun way to find Web sites related to this book. All of the sites on FactHound have been researched by our staff. *www.facthound.com*

1. Visit the FactHound home page.
2. Enter a search word related to this book, or type in this special code: 1404805958
3. Click the FETCH IT button.

Your trusty FactHound will fetch the best Web sites for you!

Index

Look for all the books in this series:

I Am a Dolphin
The Life of a Bottlenose Dolphin

I Am a Fish
The Life of a Clown Fish

I Am a Sea Turtle
The Life of a Green Sea Turtle

I Am a Seal
The Life of an Elephant Seal

I Am a Shark
The Life of a Hammerhead Shark

I Am a Whale
The Life of a Humpback Whale

MEDIA CENTER
MARLEY ELEMENTARY SCHOOL